anythink

D0821739

MATH LAB
FOR KIDS

Geometry + Topology

Fun, Hands-on Activities
for Learning Math

REBECCA RAPOPORT AND J.A. YODER

QUARRY

Brimming with creative inspiration, how-to projects, and useful information to enrich your everyday life, Quarto Knows is a favorite destination for those pursuing their interests and passions. Visit our site and dig deeper with our books into your area of interest: Quarto Creates, Quarto Cooks, Quarto Homes, Quarto Lives, Quarto Drives, Quarto Explores, Quarto Gifts, or Quarto Kids.

First Published in 2017 by Quarry Books, an imprint of The Quarto Group,
100 Cummings Center, Suite 265-D, Beverly, MA 01915, USA.
T (978) 282-9590 F (978) 283-2742 QuartoKnows.com

Quarry Books titles are also available at discount for retail, wholesale, promotional, and bulk purchase. For details, contact the Special Sales Manager by email at specialsales@quarto.com or by mail at The Quarto Group, Attn: Special Sales Manager, 401 Second Avenue North, Suite 310, Minneapolis, MN 55401, USA.

10 9 8 7 6 5 4 3 2

ISBN: 978-1-63159-454-0

Content for this book was originally found in Math Lab for Kids by Rebecca Rapoport and J.A. Yoder (Quarry Books, 2017)

Design: Laura Shaw Design, Inc
Cover Image: Alex Youngblood
Photography: Glenn Scott Photography
Illustration: J.A. Yoder & Rebecca Rapoport

Printed in USA

PUBLISHER'S NOTE Quarry Books would like to thank the staff and students at Birches School in Lincoln, Massachusetts, which graciously agreed to host the kid's photography for this book. We are especially grateful to Cecily Wardell, Director of Admissions and Placement, who generously gave our authors, art director, and photographer access to their facilities and helped us coordinate their students' participation to minimize disruption.

CONTENTS

Geometry: Learn About Shapes   5

Prisms and pyramids and Platonic solids, oh my!

Topology: Mind-Bending Shapes   21

Learn about squeezable, squishable shapes and surfaces

INTRODUCTION

This is your introduction to the gorgeous, exciting, beautiful math that only professionals see. What's truly astounding is that it's *accessible,* even to six- to ten-year-olds. We think that if more kids had a chance to play with real math, there would be far more mathematicians in the world.

Most people think you learn math by climbing a sort of ladder: first addition, then subtraction, then multiplication, then fractions, and so on. In fact, math is much more like a tree. There are many different areas of math, most of which are never seen in school. Plenty of this lovely and woefully ignored math doesn't require any previous knowledge. It's accessible to everyone, if they just knew it existed.

People who read this book sometimes ask us, "How is this math?" Kids cut and tape and sew and color. They imagine walking over bridges, reproducing the same problem that spawned an entire field of mathematics. They draw enormous shapes in parking lots. It may not look like math since there are whole chapters with no pencils or memorization or calculators—but we assure you, the math you're about to encounter is much closer to what actual mathematicians do.

Mathematicians play. They come up with interesting questions and investigate possible solutions. This often results in a lot of dead ends, but mathematicians know that failure provides a great chance to learn. In this book, you'll have a chance to think like a mathematician and experiment with a given idea to see what you can discover. That approach of just fiddling around with a problem and seeing what falls out is an extremely common and useful technique that mathematicians employ. If you take nothing else away from this book, learning to just try something—anything—and seeing what develops is a great skill for math, science, engineering, writing, and, well, life!

This is your opportunity, your gateway, into little-known worlds of math. Turn the page and explore for yourself.

HOW TO USE THIS BOOK

All of the material in this book has been successfully play-tested by six- to ten-year-olds. We do assume elementary students will have a guide (parent/teacher/older sibling) to help them work through the labs. Much of the material should be interesting to middle school, high school, and adult students. There are cases where older kids will be able to try a more advanced technique and younger kids will do something easier, or may need a little help. Younger kids may need assistance with certain labs (tying knots, threading needles, cutting with scissors, etc.).

Each section in this book contains an introductory Think About It question. The question is always related to the section's content and is meant to be played with before moving on to the labs. This gives you the opportunity to experiment with the topic before we've introduced any formal concepts. Sometimes we come back to the Think About It problem within the chapter and answer it directly. Sometimes we don't. (In that case, if you're curious, check the Hints and Solutions section.) In general, we hope students will have time to experiment and not just race through each lab. Real math is so much more about curiosity and experimentation than most people realize.

Each topic scratches the surface of a whole field of mathematics. If you're interested in more on any given topic, we've included some good sources in the Resources page.

GEOMETRY
LEARN ABOUT SHAPES

Geometry is the study of shapes. There are a lot of different ways a shape can be. It can be flat (like a circle or a square) with two dimensions—length and width. It can be solid (like a block or a ball) with three dimensions—length, width, and height. A shape can be made from lines connected at corners (mathematicians call these edges and vertices), or it can be made up of curves. A shape can have different numbers of edges and corners, or a different arrangement of curves from another shape. A shape can have different sizes.

In this chapter we'll make different types of shapes. Learning to recognize and make different kinds of shapes—to see what makes them similar and different—is a great way to start thinking about geometry and to see how we are surrounded by mathematical objects in our daily lives.

Think About It

Imagine a triangle—it's a flat shape that you can draw on a piece
of paper. Can you think of different ways you could build up a triangle
into a solid object? What could those different shapes look like?
How many can you think of?

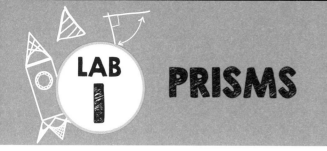
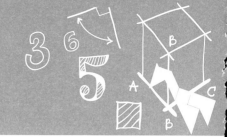
Materials

✔ Toothpicks

✔ Gumdrops

Any flat shape can be made into a prism. In this lab, we'll use toothpicks and gumdrops to create three-dimensional triangular prisms. If you mess up a gumdrop, eat it to hide the evidence!

MAKE A TRIANGULAR PRISM

1. Make a triangle with three toothpicks and three gumdrops. To make it sturdy, push the toothpicks almost all the way through the gumdrops. Then make an identical triangle. These shapes will be strongest if you put the toothpicks into the gumdrops at the correct angle and don't reposition the toothpicks. With practice, you'll get better at putting the toothpicks in at the angle you want **(fig. 1)**.

2. Take one of the triangles and lay it flat. Stick a toothpick vertically (up and down) in each gumdrop **(fig. 2)**. What shape do you notice that the points of these three toothpicks make in the air?

3. Carefully position your second triangle on top of the three toothpicks from step 2 and connect the shapes into a *triangular prism* **(fig. 3)**.

4. A prism is an *oblique prism* if the top and bottom are not directly over each other when sitting flat on the bottom. Try making an oblique triangular prism **(fig. 4)**.

MATH FACT
What's a Prism?

A *prism* is a solid shape in which the top and bottom are exactly the same, and all of the sides are rectangles.

You can also make an *oblique* prism—the top and bottom are still the same, but the prism looks like it is leaning over. Now the sides are *parallelograms* (leaning rectangles).

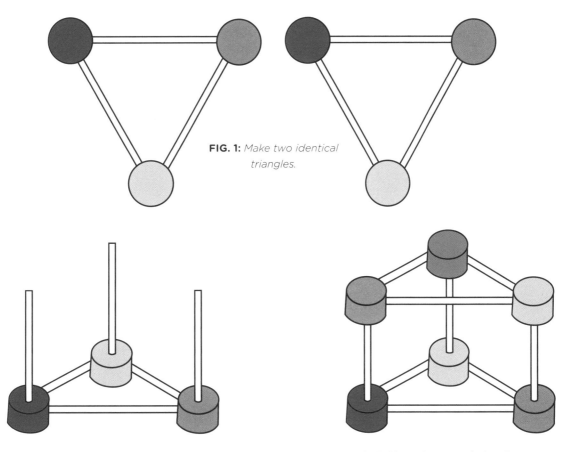

FIG. 1: *Make two identical triangles.*

FIG. 2: *Lay one of the triangles flat and stick a toothpick in each gumdrop.*

FIG. 3: *Place the second triangle on top to form a triangular prism.*

TRY THIS!

Can you make prisms starting from a four-sided shape, a five-sided shape, and a star?

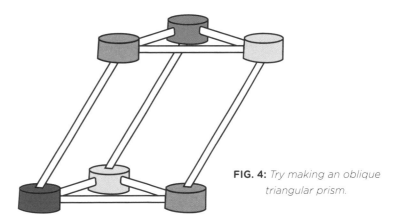

FIG. 4: *Try making an oblique triangular prism.*

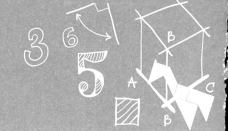
Materials

- ✔ Toothpicks
- ✔ Gumdrops
- ✔ Extra-long toothpicks, small baking skewers, or dry spaghetti or fettuccini noodles

MATH FACT

What's a Pyramid?

The Egyptian pyramids are one kind of pyramid, but there are many others. A *pyramid* is a solid shape, named after the shape of its base, which rises to a single point. All *faces* (sides) that aren't the base must be triangles, while the base can be any shape. If the *apex* (top point) of the pyramid is directly over the very center of the base so the pyramid looks like it is straight up without any lean, it is a *right pyramid*. If the pyramid is leaning, it is an *oblique pyramid*.

The three shapes above are all pyramids; the one on the right is an oblique pyramid.

Turn gumdrops and toothpicks into pyramids of all shapes and sizes!

MAKE A PYRAMID

1. Make a flat square using toothpicks and gumdrops **(fig. 1)**.

2. From each gumdrop, aim a toothpick upward at an angle so that they will all meet at a center point **(fig. 2)**.

3. Connect all the points with a single gumdrop. This is a "square pyramid," the same shape as the Egyptian pyramids **(fig. 3)**!

4. Now that you know how to make a pyramid, try making more with different base shapes, like a triangular pyramid or a pentagonal (five-sided base) pyramid **(fig. 4)**.

5. Using any base shape you want, make an oblique pyramid (it should look like it is leaning). The length of the sides going to the *apex* (top) of the pyramid will all be different, so don't use toothpicks; make the lengths you need by breaking the skewers or noodles **(fig. 5)**.

TRY THIS!

Can you make a pyramid starting from a star-shaped base? What other shapes can you turn into pyramids? Can you think of a shape that you cannot turn into a pyramid?

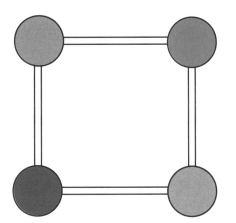

FIG. 1: *Make a flat square.*

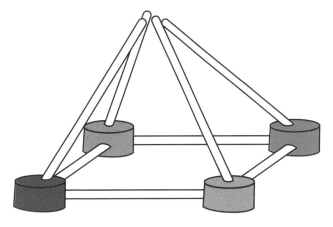

FIG. 2: *Aim a toothpick upward from each gumdrop so they meet in the center.*

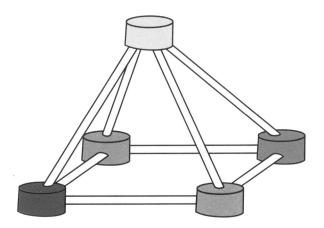

FIG. 3: *Connect all the toothpicks with a single gumdrop.*

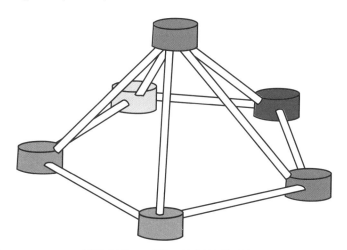

FIG. 4: *Try a different base shape.*

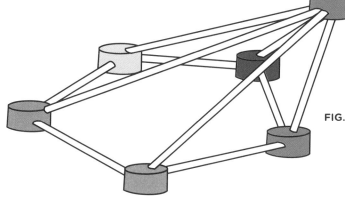

FIG. 5: *Using any base shape you want, make an oblique pyramid.*

LAB 3
ANTIPRISMS

Materials

✔ Toothpicks

✔ Gumdrops

MATH FACT

What's an Antiprism?

The two shapes at the top and bottom of an *antiprism* are connected together with a band of triangles. Looking down, you'll notice that the top and bottom shapes don't line up but instead are twisted so that the point of the top shape is above the middle of the edge of the bottom.

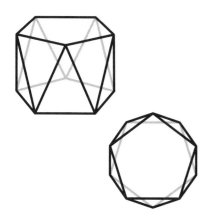

A PRISM has the same top and bottom shape, connected by rectangles or parallelograms. An ANTIPRISM also has the top and bottom shape the same, connected with triangles instead!

MAKE AN ANTIPRISM

1. Make two squares out of toothpicks and gumdrops **(fig. 1)**.

2. Hold the top square over the bottom one, then rotate it so that the corner of the top square juts out over the middle of the edge of the bottom square **(fig. 2)**.

3. We are going to make a triangle out of the corner of the top square and the edge of the bottom square. Connect this triangle with toothpicks **(fig. 3)**.

4. Moving around the shape, continue making triangles that connect the corner of one square to the edge above (or below) the other square **(fig. 4)**.

5. When you've completed the band of triangles to connect the two shapes, you've made an *antiprism*—a shape with an identical top and bottom, with all the side faces being triangles. It should look like a twisted prism **(fig. 5)**.

6. Try making a pentagonal antiprism and a triangular antiprism **(fig. 6)**. The triangular antiprism will be a challenge. Keep both—we're going to use them in Lab 4.

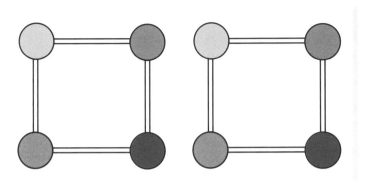

FIG. 1: *Make two squares.*

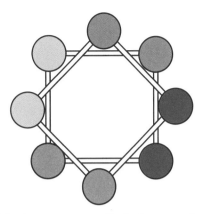

FIG. 2: *Hold the top square over the bottom one, then rotate it.*

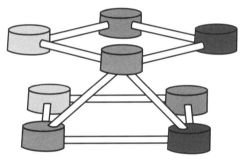

FIG. 3: *Make a triangle out of the corner of the top square and the edge of the bottom square, and then connect this triangle with toothpicks.*

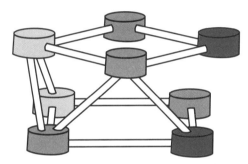

FIG. 4: *Continue making triangles that connect the corner of one square to the edge above (or below) the other square.*

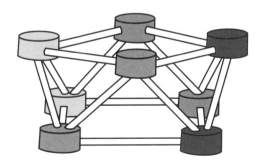

FIG. 5: *You've made an antiprism.*

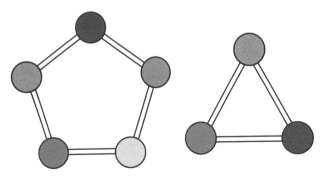

FIG. 6: *Get ready for Lab 4 by making a pentagonal antiprism (starting with a pentagon) and a triangular antiprism (starting with a triangle).*

Materials

✔ Toothpicks

✔ Gumdrops

MATH FACT

What's a Platonic Solid?

A *Platonic solid* is a solid shape that follows these rules:

- Each *face* (side) is exactly the same shape.

- Each *vertex* (corner) has exactly the same number of edges leading away from it.

- The length of every side is exactly the same.

There are only five Platonic solids: *tetrahedron, cube, octahedron, dodecahedron,* and *icosahedron.* Platonic solids are named after the Ancient Greek philosopher Plato, who described them around 350 BCE.

Tetrahedron **Cube** **Octahedron**

Dodecahedron **Icosahedron**

Just about any shape can be made into a prism or pyramid, but there are only five Platonic solids.

ACTIVITY 1: MAKE A TETRAHEDRON

1. Make a triangle from toothpicks and gumdrops **(fig. 1)**.

2. Attach toothpicks to each gumdrop aimed upward toward a center point. Connect the toothpicks with a gumdrop **(fig. 2)**.

3. Verify that all the sides have the exact same shape. Count the number of toothpicks attached to each gumdrop. Each vertex (corner) should have the same number of toothpicks attached.

This is a *tetrahedron!* In addition to being a Platonic solid, it is an example of another type of shape from this chapter. What else could this shape be called?

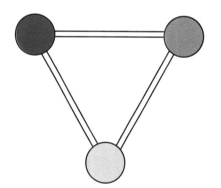

FIG. 1: *Make a triangle.*

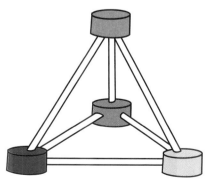

FIG. 2: *Connect a single gumdrop above the base.*

ACTIVITY 2: MAKE AN OCTAHEDRON

1. Make a square from toothpicks and gumdrops **(fig. 1)**.

2. At each gumdrop vertex, add another toothpick pointing straight up, and put a gumdrop on it **(fig. 2)**.

3. Connect the top gumdrops with toothpicks **(fig. 3)**.

This is a *cube!* In addition to being a Platonic solid, the cube is an example of another type of shape from this chapter. What else could this shape be called?

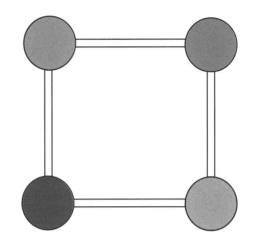

FIG. 1: *Make a square.*

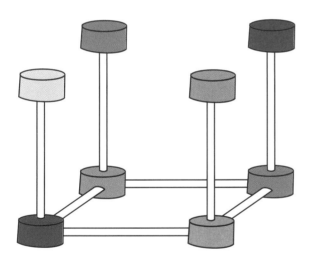

FIG. 2: *At each gumdrop vertex, add another toothpick pointing straight up, and put a gumdrop on it.*

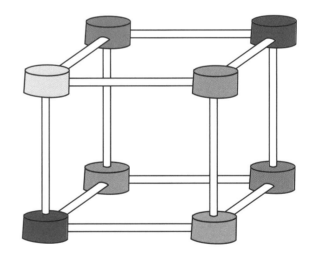

FIG. 3: *Connect the top gumdrops with toothpicks.*

Materials

✔ Heavy string (about 10 inches [25 cm] long)

✔ Scissors (to cut string)

✔ Pencil or marker

✔ Paper

✔ Tape

MATH FACT
What's a Circle?

A *circle* is a shape defined as all the points a particular distance (the *radius*) from a single point. In this activity, your string is the radius, and you move it everywhere you can around the center point to draw all the parts of the circle.

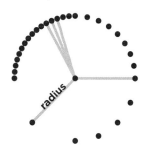

It's difficult to draw perfect shapes freehand, so people have learned to use tools to help them. Using string, tape, and a pencil, we can draw a perfect circle!

DRAW A CIRCLE

1. Use the string to tie a loose knot around the pencil, so that the string can slip down and the pencil can freely rotate. As you draw, only the very tip of your pencil should be inside this loop **(fig. 1)**.

2. Mark the center of your piece of paper. Tape the free end of your string to that spot, with the edge of your tape touching it **(fig. 2)**.

3. Draw your circle by moving the pencil as far around as you can, always keeping the string taut. If your pencil is going off your paper, make the string shorter **(fig. 3)**.

4. Practice drawing circles of different sizes by changing the length of your string. Follow the tips on the next page until you can draw perfect circles every time! You can try drawing circles with different colored markers to make a whole rainbow of circles.

FIG. 1: *Attach the string to the pencil.*

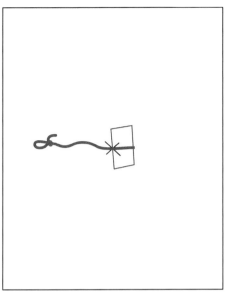

FIG. 2: *Tape the free end of your string to the center of your paper.*

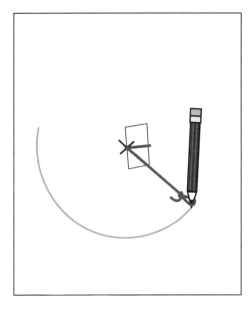

FIG. 3: *Draw a circle.*

TIPS FOR DRAWING AN ACCURATE CIRCLE

- If your string is slipping off your pencil, use a thicker string or twine. The tip of your pencil should rest in the small loop at the end of your string and drag the string along with it. If you have a thin thread, you can tape it to the end of your pencil slightly above the lead.

- Try to keep the pencil as straight up and down as you can. The more vertical your pencil is, the more accurate your circle will be.

- Make sure your tape at the center of your circle is really secure, and don't pull too hard on your string. You want the center point to stay the same the whole time you are drawing. It can help to hold down the tape with a finger.

- If you want to make more than one circle of the exact same size, mark your string at the center point. Then you can re-tape it in the same place for all the circles of that size you want to draw.

- Draw in small segments, and don't get frustrated. Every time you learn to draw something new, it takes practice!

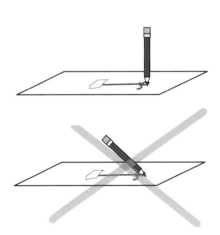

Materials

✔ Paper

✔ Pencil or marker

✔ String (about 10 inches [25 cm] long)

✔ Scissors (to cut string)

✔ Tape

MATH FACT

What's an Ellipse?

One way to define an *ellipse* is to start with two points (called *focus points*). The ellipse is made of all the points where the distance from the ellipse to the two focus points, added together, is exactly the same.

The legs from the two focus points are your string, and since your string isn't changing length as you draw the shape, you will end up with an ellipse.

A circle is a special kind of ellipse. If you make an ellipse but put the two focus points right on top of each other, you get a circle!

The total length of the red line is the same as the total length of the blue line.

We can also use string and pencil to draw special ovals called ELLIPSES. These are more challenging to draw than a circle, so be patient and try several times until you get the hang of it.

DRAW AN ELLIPSE

1. Mark two points a few inches or centimeters apart in the middle of your paper. Tape your string to the points so that the string has some slack **(fig. 1)**. For best results, arrange the tape exactly as shown.

2. To draw an ellipse, place your pencil against the string so that the string is taut, and lightly start drawing the shape **(fig. 2)**.

3. As you move around the ellipse, the string may twist. If the string twists around the pencil or the tape, that will make it shorter, and your ellipse won't be perfect. As needed, remove the pencil and reinsert it against the string to minimize twisting. Keep drawing in small segments until your ellipse is complete **(fig. 3)**.

4. Change the shape of the ellipse **(fig. 4)**. Ellipses come in lots of flavors, from very round to very oval. Try drawing ellipses starting with the focus points closer together or farther apart. Did the shape get rounder or flatter? What happens if the distance between the focus points is the same as the length of the string?

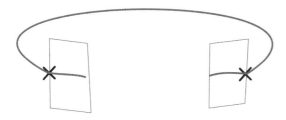

FIG. 1: *Mark two points a few inches apart. Tape your string to the points.*

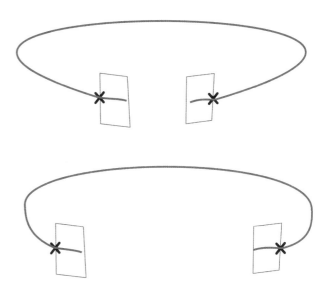

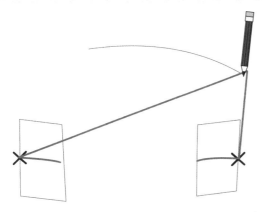

FIG. 2: *Grasp your pencil so the string is taut and lightly draw the ellipse.*

FIG. 4: *Change the shape of the ellipse by adjusting the distance between the focus points.*

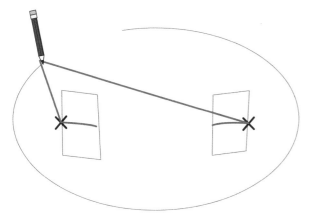

FIG. 3: *Keep drawing in small segments until your ellipse is complete.*

TIPS FOR DRAWING AN ACCURATE ELLIPSE

- Draw the ellipse in short pieces. Insert your pencil, use a light back-and-forth motion, then remove your pencil. Keep redoing this process with a new section of the ellipse until you've drawn the entire shape.

- Make sure the tape at the focus points is secure.

- If you're having trouble with your string slipping off of your pencil, use a rubber band to make a barrier to keep it in place, as close to the point of the pencil as you can.

- Keep your pencil straight up and down, not leaning.

LAB 7

DRAW GIANT CIRCLES AND ELLIPSES

Materials

✔ Sidewalk chalk

✔ Three broomsticks

✔ Packing tape, duct tape, or lots of masking tape

✔ Sturdy string, twine, or rope, at least 3 feet (92 cm) long for a circle, or 5 feet (1.5 m) for an ellipse

✔ Scissors (to cut the string)

✔ Two people for a giant circle, three for a giant ellipse

Sometimes bigger is better! We can use the same string techniques (and some friends) to draw giant circles and ellipses outside using sidewalk chalk. Make sure you have permission to draw on the sidewalk or driveway before you begin!

ACTIVITY 1: MAKE A GIANT CIRCLE

1. Make a giant "pencil" by attaching the chalk to the side of one end of a broomstick using tape. Make sure it is sturdy! You don't want your chalk to fall off **(fig. 1)**.

2. Tie a loop at each end of your string. The loops should be large enough so that you can slip the broomsticks and your giant "pencil" inside easily **(fig. 2)**.

3. Mark the center of your giant circle with chalk. (X marks the spot!) Have one person stand at the center with a broomstick and slip one loop of your string over the broomstick **(fig. 3)**. That person's job is to keep the broomstick always right over the center mark, and to stay out of the way of the string!

4. The second person should slip the other loop over the end of the giant "pencil." Then, keeping the string taut at all times, he or she will walk around the person in the middle, drawing at the same time **(fig. 4)**. He or she must keep the string taut without pulling the center off the mark, while avoiding being tangled up in the string.

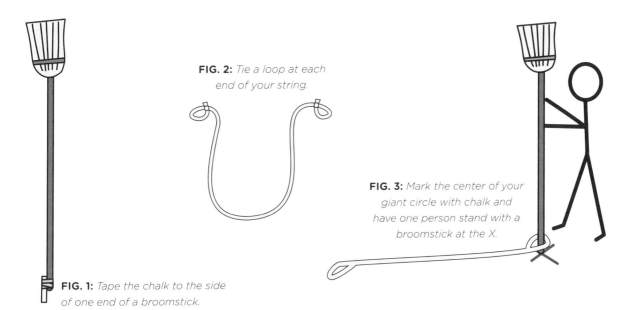

FIG. 1: *Tape the chalk to the side of one end of a broomstick.*

FIG. 2: *Tie a loop at each end of your string.*

FIG. 3: *Mark the center of your giant circle with chalk and have one person stand with a broomstick at the X.*

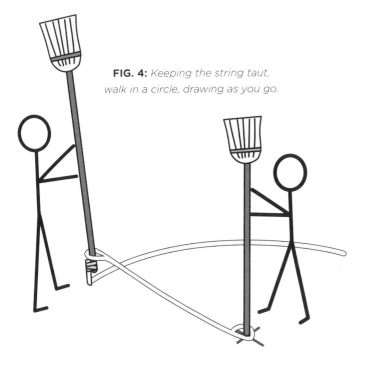

FIG. 4: *Keeping the string taut, walk in a circle, drawing as you go.*

TIPS FOR DRAWING ACCURATE GIANT SHAPES

- The "center" person needs to hold tightly to his or her broomstick so that the center doesn't slip.

- The "drawing" person needs to be careful not to pull too hard on the string; sharp tugs will pull the center away. Work together as a team!

- Try to keep the broomsticks *vertical*—straight up and down, with no lean.

- If the center broomstick slips, stop drawing until it is back in place. That's why we marked the center point(s)—so we can put it back where it belongs!

- This is truly a team effort, and it is difficult to draw an accurate giant circle or ellipse. Give everyone on your drawing team a high five when you manage to draw one.

ACTIVITY 2: *CHALLENGE!* MAKE A GIANT ELLIPSE

This one is hard! Can you (and two friends) do it?

1. Mark two points on the ground that are closer together than the length of your string.

2. Slip the ends of the looped string over the plain broomsticks (not your giant pencil). You'll need two people to hold them—one for each broomstick. Put the broomsticks on top of the marks you drew in step 1 **(fig. 1)**.

3. The third person will draw the ellipse with the giant pencil. This is best done in several short sections instead of one continuous curve; everyone is going to be dodging string and broomsticks! Just do one little piece of the ellipse at a time **(fig. 2)**.

FIG. 1: *Slip the ends of the looped string over the broomsticks and put them over the marks you drew in step 1.*

FIG. 2: *Draw the ellipse with the giant pencil, one section at a time.*

TOPOLOGY
MIND-BENDING SHAPES

Topology is one of many ways to study shapes. In topology, you can deform, or change, a shape in certain ways—by stretching, bulging, or squeezing—without turning it into a different shape. However, the rules of topology say you can't glue a shape to itself or poke a hole in it, because if you do that, you've created a new shape. Topologists study these changeable shapes to explore what other properties of a shape are still important.

Topology is also the study of spaces and how they're connected. For example, the space occupied by your house is made up of smaller spaces (rooms) connected in a particular way (doors, hallways, and so on). Topologists study knots, mazes, and lots of other interesting shapes. Their findings have helped make advances in many fields, including robotics (navigation), computer science (computer networks), biology (gene regulation), and chemistry (molecular shapes).

Think About It

**Compare a ball and a book. In what ways are their shapes different?
In what ways are they the same?**

COMPARE AND CLASSIFY SHAPES

Materials

✔ Scissors

✔ Large rubber balloon

✔ Marker

✔ A plastic sandwich bag loosely filled with clay or playdoh and then closed

✔ Paper and pencil

✔ A ball, a small bowl or box, a mug with a handle, and a bagel (or any doughnut-shaped item with a hole in the middle)

MATH MEET
Name That Shape

Topologists *classify* shapes by putting them into categories. This is a fun contest for you and some friends. In five minutes:

• Who can classify the most shapes according to their number of holes?

• Who can find at least one object with zero, one, two, three, four, and five holes?

• Who can find the object with the most holes?

• Can you find a shape that your friends won't be able to classify? Bring your confusing shapes together and see if you can figure out how many holes they have!

In topology, you can stretch, squeeze, or twist a shape without changing what kind of shape it is. We'll explore how shapes are allowed to change in topology by transforming one shape into some others.

ACTIVITY 1: TRANSFORMING A CIRCLE

1. Cut the balloon in half lengthwise so that you have a sheet of rubber.

2. With the marker, draw a circle on the rubber sheet **(fig. 1)**.

3. Try to transform the circle into a square by pulling on the edges of the rubber sheet. You might need more than two hands to do it **(fig. 2)**!

4. Can you turn the circle into a triangle by pulling on the sheet? What other shapes can you transform the circle into? Because you didn't poke a hole, cut the sheet, tape parts of it together, or draw another line, topologists consider all of these the same shape.

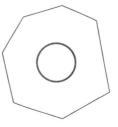

FIG. 1: *Draw a circle onto the rubber sheet.*

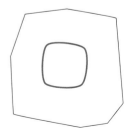

FIG. 2: *Pull on the edges of the rubber sheet to transform the circle into a square and other shapes.*

ACTIVITY 2: TRANSFORMING WITH CLAY

Next we'll use the bag of clay. Without poking a hole in the bag, or taping parts of it together, which of the shapes below can you make the bag look like?

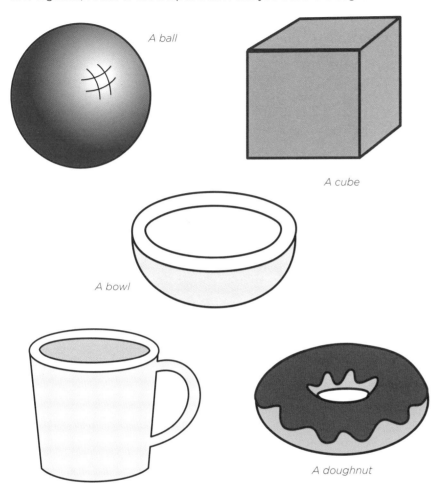

A ball

A cube

A bowl

A coffee mug with a handle

A doughnut

Which shapes could you make? To a topologist, those are the "same" shape, because they each have zero holes. How many holes are in the doughnut and the coffee mug?

Scavenger Hunt

One way topologists classify shapes is by how many holes they have. A ball has zero holes. A doughnut has one hole. A pot with a handle on each side has two holes.

Divide your paper into four sections labeled "zero," "one," "two," and "lots." Look around your house or classroom to find objects. Figure out how many holes each object has and write them on your paper.

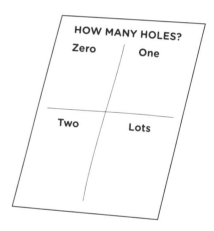

HOW MANY HOLES?

Zero	One
Two	Lots

LAB 9 · MÖBIUS STRIPS

Materials

- ✔ Four strips of white paper about 2 inches (5 cm) wide and 22 to 24 inches (56 to 61 cm) long. *You can make long strips by taping together two strips cut from one 8.5 x 11-inch (21.6 x 27.9 cm) sheet, but make sure the tape covers the whole width of the strip.*
- ✔ Tape
- ✔ Markers in at least two different colors
- ✔ Scissors

MATH FACT

What's a Möbius Strip?

A Möbius strip is a surface that has only one side and only one edge. When you draw a line down the center of a Möbius strip, you'll notice that the line goes on what used to be both sides of the original paper before you twisted it, so the line you drew is twice the length of your strip of paper!

Turn a piece of paper that has two sides and four edges into a shape that has only one side and one edge.

ACTIVITY 1: MAKE A CROWN AND A MÖBIUS STRIP

1. Before you begin, examine a strip of paper. It has two sides (front and back), and four edges (top, bottom, left, and right).

2. Make a crown by taking one strip of paper and taping the ends together, making sure there are no twists. Tape across the whole width of the strip. See if it fits smoothly on your head, like a crown **(fig. 1)**.

3. To make a Möbius strip, bring the ends of another strip of paper together (as if you're going to make another crown), then use one hand to twist one end of the strip upside down. Tape the ends together across the whole width of the strip **(fig. 2)**.

4. On your crown, carefully use a marker to draw a line down the center all the way around until the line meets up with itself. Using a different color, draw another line all the way around the inside of the crown. (You can gently turn the crown inside out to make it easier.) Notice that the crown has two "sides"—an inside and an outside—that are now marked with two different colors **(fig. 3)**.

5. Count how many edges the crown has. Does it have the same number of edges as the strip of paper you made it out of? No—a strip of paper has four edges, but the crown has only two.

6. On your Möbius strip, carefully draw a line down the center until the line meets up with itself **(fig. 4)**.

7. What do you notice about your Möbius strip? How many sides does it have? Count its edges. It should have one side and one edge—that's what makes it a Möbius strip. Can you think of any other shape that has only one edge?

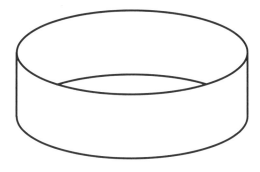

FIG. 1: *Make a crown by taping the ends of a strip of paper together.*

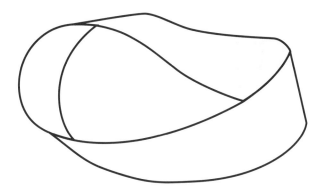

FIG. 2: *Make a Möbius strip by bringing the ends of a strip of paper together, twisting one end of the strip upside down, then taping the two ends together.*

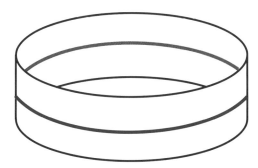

FIG. 3: *Draw a line around the center of the outside of the crown. Use a second color to draw a line around the inside.*

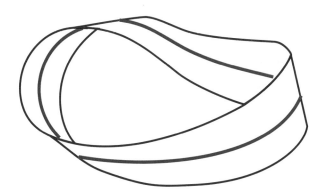

FIG. 4: *Draw a line around the center of the Möbius strip.*

MATH JOKE

Q: Why did the chicken cross the Möbius strip?

A: To get to the same side!

ACTIVITY 2: CUT THE MÖBIUS STRIP AND CROWN

1. Take your crown from Activity 1 and carefully cut down the center of the strip using the line you drew as a guide **(fig. 5)**. How many pieces did you end up with? Was it what you expected?

2. Do the same with your Möbius strip **(fig. 6)**. What happened? Was it what you expected? Is there a Möbius strip in the resulting shape(s)? How can you tell, using a marker?

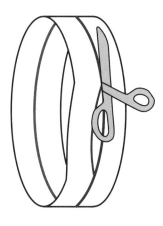

FIG. 5: *Take your crown and carefully cut down the center of the strip.*

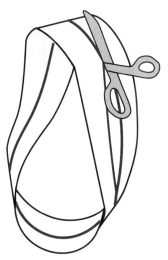

FIG. 6: *Do the same with your Möbius strip and see what happens.*

TRY THIS!

We made a Möbius strip by adding one half-twist to our paper before we taped it together. Try making rings with two half-twists, three half-twists, and four half-twists (you may need a longer strip of paper for these shapes). Using a marker, see if any of these shapes are more like our original crown or a Möbius strip. Do you see a pattern? Try cutting these strips down the middle. What happens?

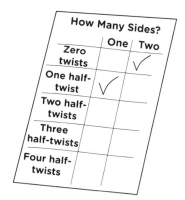

How Many Sides?		
	One	Two
Zero twists		✓
One half-twist	✓	
Two half-twists		
Three half-twists		
Four half-twists		

What's Going On?

When you cut a Möbius strip in half, you end up with a single long band that has two full twists. This band has two sides and two edges. The line you cut became the second edge. It's no longer a Möbius strip!

Counting the twists in the band can be confusing. The original Möbius strip had a half twist in it. After you cut it, each half of the original strip contributes half a twist to the final band, which accounts for one of the twists. In addition, the band is looped once around itself. When you unwind it to see the full band, that's where the second twist comes from!

Notice how the cut strip loops around itself. When you open up the band, that puts an extra twist in your final shape!

Materials

- ✔ Two strips of white paper about 2 inches (5 cm) wide and 22 to 24 inches (56 to 61 cm) long *You can make these by taping two strips cut from an 8.5 x 11-inch (21.6 x 27.9 cm) sheet together, but make sure the tape covers the whole width of the strip.*

- ✔ Tape

- ✔ Markers in at least two different colors

- ✔ Scissors

ACTIVITY 3: CUT A MÖBIUS STRIP AND CROWN INTO THIRDS

1. Make a new paper crown and a new Möbius strip with the strips of paper.

2. Carefully draw a line around the crown again, this time about a third of the way from the edge. (Don't worry if it's not exactly a third.) Using a different color, draw another line about a third of the way from the other edge **(fig. 1)**. Do the same thing with your Möbius strip **(fig. 2)**. What is different between the lines you drew on the crown and on the Möbius strip?

3. Cut the paper crown along the lines that you drew **(fig. 3)**. What shapes do you end up with?

4. Before you cut your Möbius strip into thirds, try to guess what shape or shapes you'll end up with—how many pieces, with how many twists? Once you've made your guess, cut the Möbius strip using your lines as a guide **(fig. 4)**. What do you end up with? Is it what you expected? Use a marker to figure out if any of the shapes are Möbius strips.

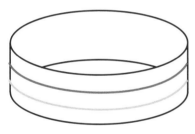

FIG. 1: *Carefully draw a line around the crown about a third of the way from each edge.*

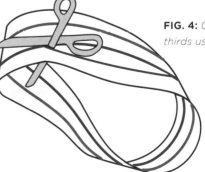

FIG. 2: *Do the same thing with your Möbius strip.*

FIG. 3: *Cut the paper crown along the lines that you drew.*

FIG. 4: *Cut the Möbius strip into thirds using your lines as a guide.*

LAB 10

MÖBIUS SURPRISE

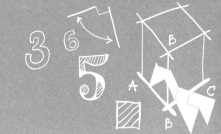

Materials

✔ Paper (8.5 x 11 inches [21.6 x 27.9 cm])

✔ Markers in two different colors

✔ Tape

✔ Scissors

TRY THIS!

The Möbius surprise is made by connecting a ring and a Möbius strip and cutting them. Try inventing other combinations of shapes and twists, cutting them, and seeing what you end up with. Can you invent a surprise shape named after you?

Martin Gardner, a mathematician famous for introducing fun mathematical challenges to the public, invented an entertaining surprise using the concepts we just learned. Try it for yourself!

TRY THE MÖBIUS SURPRISE

1. Draw a thick plus sign on a piece of white paper. Cut out the shape. Draw a single solid line across the short arm of the plus sign. Turn the shape over, and draw the same line on the back. Draw two dotted vertical lines dividing the long arm of the plus sign into equal widths. Turn the shape over and repeat these lines on the back of the paper **(fig. 1)**.

2. Take the two horizontal arms, with the single solid line on them, and tape the edges together without any twists to form a ring. Make sure the tape goes all the way across the joint so that it won't fall apart later **(fig. 2)**.

3. Take the remaining two arms and tape them into a Möbius strip opposite your original ring **(fig. 3)**.

4. Before you cut along your lines, try to guess what the final shape will be **(fig. 5)**. Will it be a giant ring? Several interlocked rings? Some other shape?

5. The order that you cut the lines is important. First, cut along the dotted lines (they should be on the twisted ring of the surprise). Next, cut along the solid line **(fig. 4)**. What do you end up with?

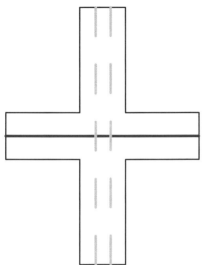

FIG. 1: *Cut out the shape of a plus sign. Draw the horizontal and vertical cutting lines on both sides of the paper.*

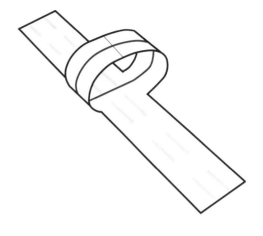

FIG. 2: *Tape the short arms.*

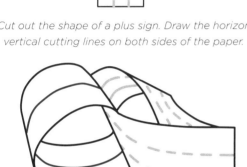

FIG. 3: *Tape the long arms into a Möbius strip.*

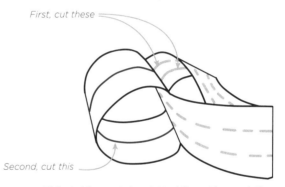

First, cut these

Second, cut this

FIG. 4: *First cut the dotted lines, then cut the solid line.*

FIG. 5: *Before cutting the lines, guess the result!*

HINTS AND SOLUTIONS

I. GEOMETRY: LEARN ABOUT SHAPES

Think About It: There are lots of ways to make a 3D shape from a triangle. A triangular prism is like a really thick triangle, and if you look at it from above it looks like a triangle.. A pyramid takes a shape and raises it up in a point, so that if you look at it from the side it looks like a triangle. There are lots of 3D shapes with triangle faces.

LAB 1, Try this!:

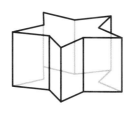

Prisms starting from a four-sided shape, a five-sided shape, and a star.

LAB 2, Try this!:

A pyramid starting from a star-shaped base. Shapes that you cannot turn into a pyramid include a circle, figure eight, and more you might think of.

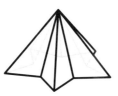

LAB 3

Triangular antiprism

Pentagonal antiprism

LAB 4, Octahedron: Some ways in which the octahedron is different from the tetrahedron: Octahedron: 8 sides, 6 vertices, 12 edges. Tetrahedron: 4 sides, 4 vertices, 6 edges. Every corner of the octahedron connects to four triangles. Every corner of the tetrahedron connects to three triangles. Compare the octahedron you built to the triangular antiprism that you built in Lab 3, step 6. What do you notice? They're the same shape!

2. TOPOLOGY: MIND-BENDING SHAPES

LAB 8

- **Activity 1, step 4:** Yes, you can make a triangle and many other shapes.

- **Activity 2:** You can stretch or squeeze the bag to make it look like a ball, cube, or bowl, but not like a doughnut or mug.

- **Scavenger Hunt *hint*:** Here are some examples of objects in each category to get you started.

  1. No holes: book, plate, cup (no handles)

  2. One hole: cup with handle, CD, bead

  3. Two holes: unzipped coat, grocery bag (if it has two handles)

  4. More than two holes: sieve, slatted chair, sweater

LAB 9

- **Activity 1, step 7:** The Möbius strip has one edge.

- **Activity 2, step 1:** You end up with two crowns.

- **Activity 2, step 2:** You end up with a single long band that has two full twists.

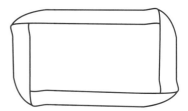

- **Activity 3, step 2:** If you draw a line on the crown, the other side of the crown (inside) is blank. For the Möbius strip, there are no blank places. (There is only one side.)

- **Activity 3, step 3:** You end up with three crowns.

- **Activity 3, step 4:**

Try this!:

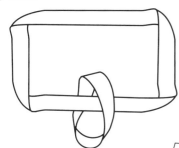

You end up with a long band with multiple twists interlinked with a small Möbius strip.

You should get these results.

How Many Sides?		
	One	**Two**
Zero twists		✓
One half twist	✓	
Two half twist		✓
Three half twist	✓	
Four half twist		✓

LAB 10

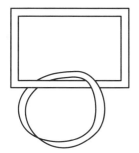

This is the shape you will get when you cut. Surprised?

RESOURCES

Go to **mathlabforkids.com** or **quartoknows.com/page/math-lab** for printable versions of some exercises and pull-out pages in this book.

National Council of Teachers of Mathematics
There is some great material in the "Classroom Resources" section. www.nctm.org

Fractal Foundation
Check out the Fractivities and other content in the Explore Fractals section. http://fractalfoundation.org

Zome
Geometric building toy. http://zometool.com

ACKNOWLEDGMENTS

Rebecca would like to thank her parents, Ron and Joan, for teaching her to write clearly, concisely, and grammatically correctly. And a second round of thanks to her father for making her think writing a book is a normal thing to do.

She would also like to thank her husband, Dean, for his support throughout the process.

Rebecca's fabulous eldest child, Allanna, caused her to realize this book needed to be written. Allanna and her brother, the forever inquisitive Zack, were not only enthusiastic about the idea of Mom writing a book but also cheerfully play-tested some of the book's content. Rebecca looks forward to working through all the labs with her youngest, Xander, when he's old enough. In the meantime, she appreciates the good humor and joy all three bring into her life every day.

We would both like to acknowledge how much fun it was to work on this book together. It was a great collaborative effort and resulted in something we're both proud of. The book also gave us a wonderful opportunity to continue the meaningful work we began at the STEAM (science, technology, engineering, art, and math) after-school enrichment center we helped build.

J.A. would like to thank Rebecca for her patience, her enthusiasm, and for the opportunity for this collaboration that taught each of us some new things and strengthened our long-time friendship. This was a wonderful chance to improve my own ideas by bouncing them off someone I trust, learn a bunch of really cool new stuff (whether it made it into the book or not!), and share many truly terrible math jokes.

We owe a big debt of gratitude to all the people who helped us test and hone the book's content, especially the staff and students of Birches School in Lincoln, Massachusetts, whose cheerful faces brighten up this book's pages.

J.A.'s math professor mother, Kathie, provided valuable feedback on the book's content and her enthusiasm in working every lab made us happy.

Of course, we'd like to thank our editor, Joy, and Tiffany for pitching the book idea to us and Quarry in the first place. Meredith and Anne were invaluable in making this book look as good as it does.

Finally, we'd like to thank all the staff at Quarry Books who worked on this book for helping us put such a beautiful, full-color romp through math out into the world.

ABOUT THE AUTHORS

Rebecca Rapoport holds degrees in mathematics from Harvard and Michigan State. From her first job out of college, as one of the pioneers of Harvard's Internet education offerings, she has been passionate about encouraging her love of math in others.

As an early contributor to both retail giant Amazon.com and Akamai Technologies, the No. 1 firm in cloud computing, Rapoport played a key role in several elements of the Internet revolution.

Rapoport returned to her first love, education, as an innovator of new methods to introduce children and adults to the critically important world of STEM as COO of Einstein's Workshop, an enrichment center dedicated to helping kids explore the creative side of science, technology, engineering, art, and math. One of their classes for six- to ten-year-olds is Recreational Math, which inspired the creation of this book.

Currently, Rapoport is developing and teaching innovative math curricula at Boston-area schools.

J.A. Yoder holds a degree in computer science from Caltech. She is an educator and engineer who has a lifetime love of puzzles and patterns. Her educational philosophy is that hands-on creative work is both the most fun and the most effective way to learn. She developed and taught the original hands-on-math lessons for an after-school program that eventually inspired this book. Some of her happiest memories come from "eureka moments"—either from learning something that makes a dozen other things suddenly make sense, or the sense of accomplishment that comes from solving a clever puzzle. The only thing better is sharing this joy with others.